ENF

W9-CFA-152

MISSOURI

Pamela McDowell

www.av2books.com

LET'S READ
AV2
BY WEIGL™
ADDED VALUE • AUDIO VISUAL

AV² provides enriched content that supplements and complements this book. Weigl's AV² books strive to create inspired learning and engage young minds in a total learning experience.

Your AV² Media Enhanced books come alive with...

 Audio
Listen to sections of the book read aloud.

 Video
Watch informative video clips.

 Embedded Weblinks
Gain additional information for research.

 Try This!
Complete activities and hands-on experiments.

 Key Words
Study vocabulary, and complete a matching word activity.

 Quizzes
Test your knowledge.

 Slide Show
View images and captions, and prepare a presentation.

... and much, much more!

Go to **www.av2books.com**, and enter this book's unique code.

BOOK CODE

E 8 9 8 9 6 4

AV² by Weigl brings you media enhanced books that support active learning.

Published by AV² by Weigl
350 5th Avenue, 59th Floor
New York, NY 10118
Website: www.av2books.com   www.weigl.com

Library of Congress Cataloging-in-Publication Data
McDowell, Pamela.
 Missouri / Pamela McDowell.
    p. cm. -- (Explore the U.S.A.)
 Includes bibliographical references and index.
 ISBN 978-1-61913-369-3 (hard cover : alk. paper)
 1. Missouri--Juvenile literature. I. Title.
 F466.3.M33 2012
 977.8--dc23
                    2012015094

Printed in the United States of America in North Mankato, Minnesota
1 2 3 4 5 6 7 8 9   16 15 14 13 12

052012
WEP040512

Project Coordinator: Karen Durrie
Art Director: Terry Paulhus

Weigl acknowledges Getty Images as the primary image supplier for this title.

2

MISSOURI

Contents

3

This is Missouri.
It is called the Show Me State.
This means people in Missouri think
people must show what they can do.

6

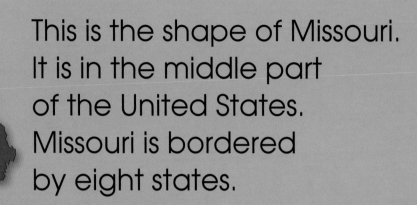

This is the shape of Missouri. It is in the middle part of the United States. Missouri is bordered by eight states.

Where is Missouri?

N
W E
S

Canada

United States

Pacific Ocean

Atlantic Ocean

Mexico

The Mississippi River makes the east border of Missouri.

The Pony Express started in Missouri more than 150 years ago. Men rode horses to deliver mail.

The Pony Express Trail was 2,000 miles long.

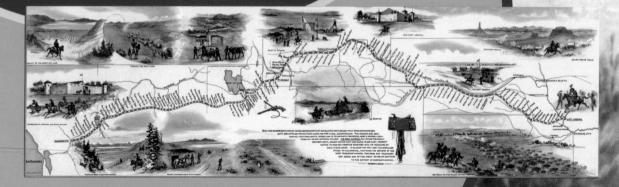

The white hawthorn blossom
is the Missouri state flower.
Sour berries grow on these bushes.

The Missouri state seal has
two grizzly bears holding a shield.

The grizzly bears
stand for strength.

This is the Missouri state flag. It has the state seal and three stripes.

The red stripe stands for bravery.

The state animal of Missouri is the Missouri Mule. Farmers and soldiers used mules for their strength.

Mules pulled many pioneer wagons west.

This is the state capital of Missouri. It is named Jefferson City. This city was named after Thomas Jefferson.

Thomas Jefferson was the third president of the United States.

Hay, corn, oats, and rice grow in Missouri. There are more than 100,000 farms in the state.

There are more cows and hogs than people in some parts of Missouri.

Missouri is known for the St. Louis Gateway Arch.
It is taller than any building in St. Louis.
People can ride to the top of the Arch.

MISSOURI FACTS

These pages provide detailed information that expands on the interesting facts found in the book. These pages are intended to be used by adults as a learning support to help young readers round out their knowledge of each state in the *Explore the U.S.A.* series.

Pages 4–5

Missouri is named for the river that flows through it. The state's nickname may come from Congressman Willard Vandiver's 1899 speech. He said, "I come from a state that raises corn and cotton and cockleburs and Democrats, and frothy eloquence neither convinces me nor satisfies me. I am from Missouri. You have got to show me."

Pages 6–7

On August 10, 1821, Missouri became the 24th state to join the United States. At that time, Missouri was called the Gateway to the West. Many pioneers traveled through Missouri on their way west. Missouri is located in Tornado Alley and gets about 25 tornadoes a year. Missouri is bordered by Iowa, Illinois, Kentucky, Tennessee, Arkansas, Oklahoma, Kansas, and Nebraska.

Pages 8–9

The Pony Express made communication between the east and west faster. On the first day of service, riders on horses carrying saddlebags filled with mail were dispatched from St. Joseph, Missouri, and Sacramento, California. More than 100 stations, 80 riders, and about 500 horses made up the Pony Express. After 19 months, the service ended when the Pacific Telegraph line was built.

Pages 10–11

After the white hawthorn blooms, it grows small berries that look like apples. This fruit can be made into jam or tea. The grizzly bears on the Missouri state seal are symbols of strength and courage. The shield has the U.S. coat of arms on one side. On the other side, the crescent moon and grizzly bear are symbols of Missouri.

Pages 12–13

The state flag was approved in 1913. The red stripe symbolizes bravery, the white stripe means purity, and the blue stripe stands for justice. The 24 stars around the seal represent that Missouri was the 24th state to join the United States.

Pages 14–15

The Missouri Mule became the official state animal in 1995. Mules were used by pioneers to pull wagons in the 1800s. They also moved soldiers and supplies in World Wars I and II. For many years, Missouri produced the most mules in the country. Mules are made by breeding female horses with male donkeys.

Pages 16–17

Jefferson City became the state capital in 1821. Before then, St. Louis and St. Charles had each served as the capital. Jefferson City has a population of just over 40,000. The Missouri River flows through Jefferson City and then to St. Louis. Jefferson City began as a small, remote trading post.

Pages 18–19

Soybeans have become the most valuable crop in Missouri. About 5 million acres (2 million hectares) of soybeans are harvested in Missouri every year. Missouri also has some of the world's largest deposits of lead. Cars, airplanes, soft drinks, electronics, and chemicals are also made in Missouri.

Pages 20–21

The St. Louis Gateway Arch was built to honor explorers and settlers who started in St. Louis for points west. It was completed in 1965. The Arch contains 900 tons (816 tonnes) of stainless steel, and weighs 17,246 tons (15,565 tonnes). It is 630 feet (192 meters) tall. The arch is part of the Jefferson National Expansion Memorial, which honors Thomas Jefferson and the Louisiana Purchase.

WORD LIST

Research has shown that as much as 65 percent of all written material published in English is made up of 300 words. These 300 words cannot be taught using pictures or learned by sounding them out. They must be recognized by sight. This book contains 51 common sight words to help young readers improve their reading fluency and comprehension. This book also teaches young readers several important content words, such as proper nouns. These words are paired with pictures to aid in learning and improve understanding.

Page	Sight Words First Appearance
4	can, do, in, is, it, me, means, must, people, show, state, the, they, think, this, what
7	by, makes, of, part, river, where
8	long, men, miles, more, than, to, was, years
11	a, for, grow, has, on, these, two, white
12	and, three
15	animal, many, their, used
16	after, city, named
19	farms, some, there
20	any

Page	Content Words First Appearance
4	Missouri
7	border, shape, United States
8	horses, mail, Pony Express, trail
11	berries, bushes, flower, grizzly bears, blossom, seal, shield
12	bravery, flag, stripes
15	farmers, mule, soldiers, strength, wagons
16	capital, president, Thomas Jefferson
19	corn, cows, hay, hogs, oats, rice
20	building, Gateway Arch, St. Louis, top

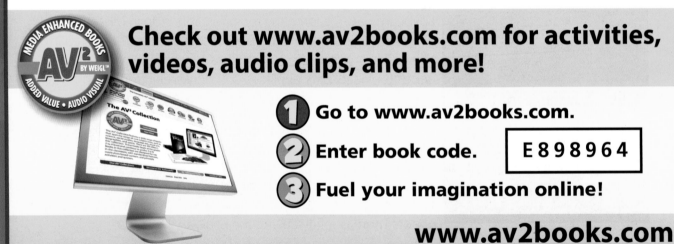